LET'S LEARN SKI TOURING:

Your Guide to

CROSS-COUNTRY FUN

LET'S LEARN

IN THIS

SERIES

LET'S LEARN

TO SKI

•

LET'S LEARN

TO SNORKEL

 **WALKER AND COMPANY, New York**

SKI TOURING:

Your Guide to CROSS-COUNTRY FUN

by GENE TINKER

Thank you . . .

to Bob Barton, General Manager of the Woodstock Inn's Ski Touring Center in Vermont—where most of these photos were taken—for assisting in every conceivable way in the taking of photographs, and for providing models and equipment on very short notice. Thanks also to John Greene, formerly a member of the U.S. Nordic Team and now with Bass Sports. John gave generously of his time and advice, and Bass Sports supplied the skiing equipment used in these photos.

THIS ONE IS
FOR
BARBARA

First published in the United States of America in 1971 by the Walker Publishing Company, Inc.

Published simultaneously in Canada by Fitzhenry & Whiteside, Limited, Toronto.

Trade ISBN: 0-8027-6089-9
Reinf. ISBN: 0-8027-6090-2

Library of Congress Catalog Card Number: 73-169255

All photos by the author
Designed by Carl Weiss

Printed in the United States of America.

CONTENTS

Ski touring is a great way for the whole
family to explore the countryside.

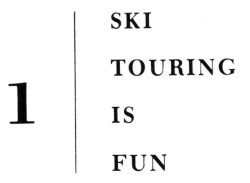

1 | SKI TOURING IS FUN

Ski touring is fun. It is a great way to enjoy the outdoors in wintertime and it is so easy to do that it can be enjoyed equally by children and adults.

Ski touring is an uncomplicated sport. Equipment is simple and low in cost, and techniques are easy to master. And unlike Alpine skiing, it's where you go and what you see on a touring trip that brings you enjoyment, rather than how gracefully or how fast you ski.

Touring gets you out into the woods and fields, away from noise and crowds and civilization. Because you can ski anywhere that you can find a snow-covered surface, you can take pleasure in such simple things as a picnic in the woods or in just enjoying the scenery, far away from the distractions of daily life.

One recent advertisement for touring equipment tells the whole story: "If you're old enough to walk and young enough to dance, you've got what it takes to enjoy ski touring." Learning to tour on skis is easy and it doesn't matter how

Open fields, unplowed country roads, golf courses—just about
any snow-covered surface can be explored on touring skis.

young or old you are.

Experienced ski tourers usually go with at least one other person. One reason is that almost any pleasure is more enjoyable when shared. Another reason is that it just makes sense not to go off into the woods or to make a long ski touring trip alone, any more than it would make sense to take a summertime hike alone deep into the woods or mountains.

Ski touring is especially enjoyable as a family activity. You can enjoy touring with any member of your family old enough to walk, regardless of age.

Speed is not important in touring. Indeed, touring is a way of "slowing down" and enjoying the scenery around you. When you go on a trip through the woods or fields, you will find time to notice things you hadn't seen before, such as beautiful views, winter birds, and the wintertime pattern of life that is written on the snow by the creatures that live in the wild.

A touring trip is as long as you make it. You can go out for just an hour or so, or a half-day, or even overnight if you have the necessary camping equipment.

Where Can You Go Ski Touring? You can tour on just about any snow-covered surface. Golf courses, old abandoned logging roads, farm fields, hiking trails, wooded areas, and jogging and bicycle paths are all suitable. Snow-covered public parks and even your own backyard—if it is big enough—are great places to practice. Make sure to obtain permission before skiing over someone else's land. Just because another's property is covered with snow, it doesn't mean you can trespass.

One way of finding a good place for touring is to contact the Ski Touring Council, West Hill Road, Troy, Vermont 05868. The Council is a non-profit organization interested in encouraging people to try ski touring. They have a list of trails and each year they sponsor several instruction sessions, which are open to everyone.

The different kinds of skiing

Skiing on snow is divided into two general classifications: Alpine skiing and Nordic skiing. Nordic skiing is a term which describes ski jumping, ski touring, and cross-country skiing. The equipment and techniques for each are quite different.

Alpine Skiing (also called downhill skiing): Alpine skiing is a very exciting and increasingly popular sport which was developed in the Alpine countries of Europe. The enjoyment is derived from skiing fast, under control, downhill. This variety of skiing is done at developed ski areas, where there are lifts or tows which transport skiers to the top of the mountain. Once at the top, the skiers then ski more or less straight down the slope.

Alpine skis are wider and heavier than touring skis. They are made of wood,

Ski touring centers, such as the Woodstock Ski Touring Center in Woodstock, Vermont, are excellent sources of information on touring technique and trails. Equipment can be rented or purchased at these centers.

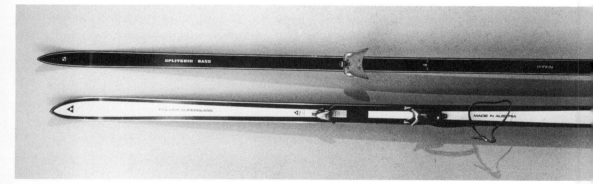

Above, is a modern high-performance Alpine ski, the Fischer Superglass. The Alpine bindings are the step-in variety, and are designed to hold the skier's toe and heel securely to the ski until a preset amount of torque is applied, as happens in a fall. These skis have very hard steel edges and high-density polyethylene bottoms. The Splitkein/Bass touring ski, top, is much lighter and narrower than an Alpine ski. It is constructed of laminated wood. Wax is applied to the wooden running surface to enable the tourer to ski uphill as well as downhill. The light Eie/Bass binding consists of a toepiece which holds only the toe of the ski boot to the ski. The metal device mounted in back of the toepiece is designed to prevent the skier's heel from sliding sideways, but it does not actually fasten the heel to the ski.

fiberglass, metal, or combinations of these materials. They have steel edges which make turning easy, and their bottoms are of a special plastic which seldom needs waxing.

Alpine bindings are very ruggedly constructed. They hold down the heel as well as the toe of the ski boot. When a certain amount of force is applied, such as during a fall, they release the boot to prevent injuries to the skier.

Alpine boots are made of leather or plastic, or a combination of these materials. Plastic boots are rapidly becoming the most popular. These boots are very stiff and high. They are designed for one purpose: skiing downhill. They are not especially easy to use when walking.

Alpine ski poles are made, in most cases, of either aluminum or steel. For most skiing situations, the best length is the distance from the floor to just under the skier's armpit.

Nordic Skiing is the term used to describe the kinds of skiing which were developed in the Nordic countries. They are recreational ski touring, competitive cross-country skiing, and ski jumping. Ski touring is the term used to describe touring across country on skis, just for fun.

Cross-country skiing is a term generally used to describe racing. In this activity, highly trained skiers race over a measured course to see who can cover the course in the shortest time. Sometimes, people refer to ski touring as cross-country skiing. In this book, we will refer to these two activities as we describe them here.

Ski jumping is a competitive event performed on a specially designed jumping hill. The competitors use special jumping skis and boots, and are scored on the distance jumped as well as their form while in the air.

Touring skis are narrow and light. Most models are made of wood, although fiberglass skis are now being introduced by some manufacturers. Since turning is not done as it is in Alpine skiing, steel edges are not required. Touring skis must be waxed to permit you to ski up and down hills.

Touring bindings are very light and are designed to hold only the toes of the boots. It is important to be able to raise your heel when touring and it is for this reason that Alpine bindings would not be suitable.

Touring boots are much lighter and more flexible than Alpine boots. Some types are cut high and cover the ankle, but the lower-cut models, until recently thought of as racing boots, are becoming increasingly popular for general recreational use.

Touring poles are usually of bamboo. (Racers often use specially made aluminum poles.) They are lighter and slightly longer than Alpine poles, and have a curved point at the lower end.

Ski touring differs from Alpine skiing as much as ping-pong differs from tennis. Neither activity is especially better or more fun than the other—they are both enjoyable, each in its different way. The purpose of this book is to show you how to enjoy yourself on touring skis.

The NASTAR (National Standard Races) program offers amateur recreational skiers of all ages a taste of cross-country ski racing. These racers are participating in a NASTAR race at the Woodstock Ski Touring Center in Woodstock, Vermont. ▶

Modern ski touring boots are built more like shoes than like ski boots. The Rosemount Fastback Alpine ski boot, top, provides the firm support required for Alpine skiing. The Bass touring boot, below, is low-cut and flexible. It features an elastic cuff, which helps to keep the snow out when skiing through deep powder. Both boots are excellent pieces of equipment for the activities for which they were designed.

2 | EQUIPMENT YOU WILL NEED

Touring equipment is available in a variety of styles and brands. Each year as touring becomes more popular, the selection becomes greater. The purpose of this chapter is to help you to choose equipment that is just right for you.

Many beginners prefer to rent their equipment for the first trip or two, until they find out whether or not they will enjoy touring. If you decide to rent before you buy, the following should be of interest.

How To Find A Rental Shop: You can find a rental shop by checking out the advertisements in *Skiing* and *Ski* magazines, or by looking in the Yellow Pages of the telephone book. If you live in or near the snow belt, your newspaper will probably carry advertisements placed by ski shops. Another source of information is your friends, if you have any who like touring.

What You Can Expect From Rental Equipment: While you can't expect the gear you rent to be brand-new, it should be in good condition. Examine it carefully when you rent. It should not show signs of abuse; the skis should not be warped; and the bindings should be securely mounted. Check the poles to make sure the straps and baskets are securely fastened and that the shafts are not splintered. The boots should be comfortable, flexible, and waterproof.

A rental shop should wax your skis for you before your first day's trip. If you rent your equipment for more than a day, you can't expect the shop to wax your skis each day you use them. However, they should wax them for the conditions which exist on the day you rent them.

Buying equipment

When you decide to buy touring equipment, do so at a professional ski shop.

[8]

Touring poles are generally constructed of bamboo. They are very light in weight. At the top end is a handle with a strap. At the lower end is a ring—called a basket—and a curved steel tip. The function of the basket is to prevent the pole from sinking too far into the snow. The better quality touring skis are purchased separately from the bindings. They are made of laminated wood, although fiberglass touring skis are beginning to make an appearance. Bindings are designed to hold the toe of the boot. Touring boots are flexible, comfortable, and light.

Touring equipment can be rented at many professional ski touring centers staffed by knowledgeable experts who will make sure you get the equipment best suited to your age, height, physical condition, and experience—or lack of it.

These specialty stores are staffed by experienced skiers who can give you good advice.

It is important to remember to buy equipment which is suitable to your age, size, and ability, rather than equipment which you might have seen used by a well-known racer. Your requirements are far different from those of a racer. The sales clerks in a good ski shop will make sure the equipment you buy is just right for you.

You can find a pro ski shop in the same ways listed for finding a rental shop. If you rented equipment before buying, you can buy your gear from the same shop.

When you buy equipment, take your time. Make sure that you fully understand the instructions given to you by the sales clerk. Don't hesitate to come back to the shop if you have further questions. Professionals who operate ski shops are interested in making sure that your ski touring is successful. They always welcome your questions on equipment, techniques, or places where you can go touring.

Skis: Most touring skis are constructed of wood—although some are of fiberglass. Touring skis are slightly wider and heavier than cross-country racing skis; but they are much lighter and narrower than Alpine skis. They will last for years if properly cared for.

The function of your skis is to float you over the snow. It is the length of your skis, not their width, which permits you to skim over the snow's surface. So, if you have had some experience in Alpine skiing, do not be concerned because your touring skis seem narrow.

Choosing skis of proper length is easy. As shown in the photo, stand upright and put your arm up above your head. If the ski comes up to the palm of your hand, it is the right length.

It is important to take your time when buying skis and other equipment. Make sure the salesman explains the merits of the various kinds of equipment.

To find the ski of the proper length, stand upright, raise your arm above your head, and place the ski next to your arm. If the tip of the ski reaches to the palm of your hand, it will be the right length. In the photo above, the ski might be a little short for the skier.

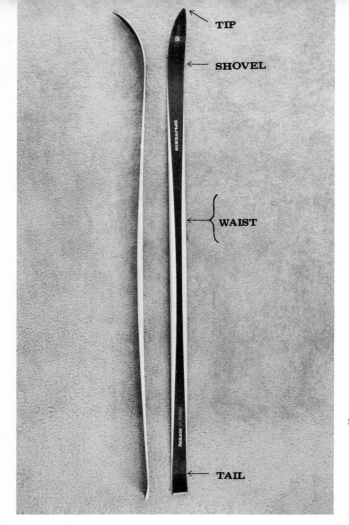

Parts of the ski are: tip, shovel, waist, tail.

The front end of your ski is called the tip. The up-curved part is called the shovel. The middle section is the waist, and the back end is called the tail.

Touring skis cost considerably less than Alpine skis. You can buy a pair of touring skis for as little as $20.00. As with many things, however, you get what you pay for. While high-quality skis will cost more, they will also perform better and last longer.

You will probably come across some low-cost touring sets, particularly in children's sizes, which have bindings pre-mounted on the skis. These pre-packaged sets cost very little, but have no durability. However, they are sometimes used for getting children started touring.

The better-quality skis do not have pre-mounted bindings. The skis and bindings are purchased separately. The bindings should be mounted by a professional.

You will notice a groove running the length of the bottoms of your skis. It is there to make it easy for you to ski in a straight line when you are going downhill. Without the grooves, your skis would tend to skid from side to side on a downhill run.

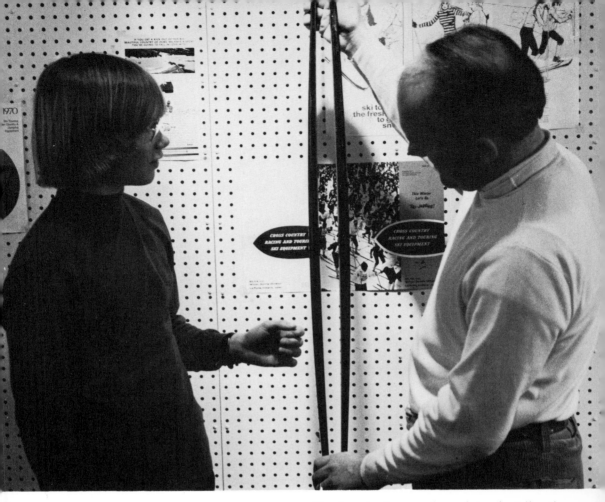

Camber is the word used to describe the curve that is built into a pair of skis. It is important to have the right amount of camber —enough to distribute your weight over the entire length of the ski when you are standing on it. If your skis have too much camber, your weight will be concentrated at the shovels and tails. If they have too little, your weight will be concentrated near the waists of the skis.

The photo at left shows why it is necessary for touring boots to be flexible. This young skier is walking up a slight hill, and raises her heels with each step. If her heels were secured to her skis, as they would be in Alpine skiing, she would not be able to walk properly.

The Alpine boot, right, is high, stiff, and sometimes, as with the Rosemount Fastback shown here, has a provision for adjusting the degree of forward lean. These boots are used by advanced skiers and are designed for one purpose: skiing downhill. They are not designed for walking. The touring boot, left, is low-cut and is comfortable for walking as well as touring.

Boots: Until recently, tourers used boots that came up to their ankles or over them. Today, however, many tourers prefer low-cut boots, because they are lighter and less tiring to use. They look rather like men's or boy's shoes. They are quite flexible and are made of leather or leather/synthetic combinations. Racing boots are low-cut too, but they are lighter in weight than touring boots.

Choose boots with a sealed sole. They should also be waterproof. With proper care, they will last for years. Children usually outgrow their boots before they wear them out.

Comfort is essential. When buying your boots, keep them on your feet for at least ten or fifteen minutes. Flex them and walk around in the ski shop, to make certain that they fit well. Try on several different types. Make sure the pair you buy is the most comfortable for you.

Boots can cost as little as $12.00. But if you have to economize in buying touring gear, do not economize on your boots. Buy the best you can possibly afford. Economize on some other article of equipment. It is better to get an expensive pair of boots which will fit well—and give years of use—than it is to save a few dollars by buying a cheap pair. A good pair will cost between $20.00 and $30.00.

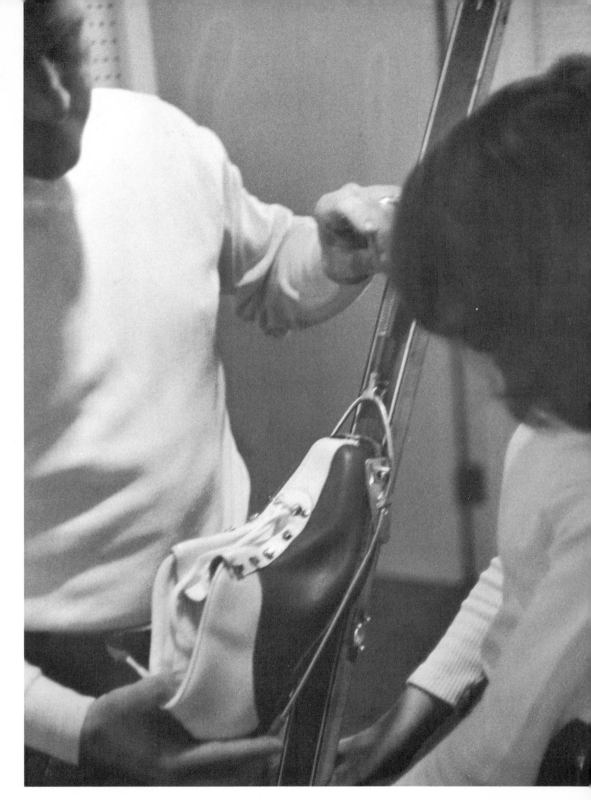

The touring boots shown here are the high-cut models, which cover the ankle. Until recently, these were thought of as the only boots suitable for touring. Now, however, recreational skiers have begun using the low-cut models and find them quite satisfactory.

The Eie bindings shown above feature a spring on the toe plate. Metal fittings on the Eie boots are engaged by this spring when the skier steps into the bindings. The spring is released simply by pushing down on its front end with your hand or your ski pole.

You might well wonder how you will keep snow out of your boots if they are cut low, below the ankle. Gaiters, or spats, are the answer. These handy, elastic-topped accessories fit over your boots and ankles and seal out the snow. Some boots, such as the Bass Eie boot, have elastic tops which seal out the snow.

Bindings: Bindings are metal devices which hold your boots securely to your skis. They are most often made of aluminum. They are designed to permit your heel to move up and down freely; thus, they fasten only to the toe of your boot.

There are several types of bindings on the market and new ones are introduced almost every year. One popular type is the Eie. It is a "step-in" binding. A spring on the binding clicks into a metal plate on the toe of the boot, which holds the boot to the ski. This step-in design makes it easy to get in and out of the binding.

Another widely used brand is the Rottefella binding. This is a popular and reliable binding which has proven to be dependable over the many years it has been on the market. A curved, toothed device, mounted just forward of the boot plate, is hooked to the clamp that secures the toe of your boot to the ski. Vertical pegs on the boot plate of the binding fit into holes drilled into the forward ends of the soles of your boots.

The Eie and Rottefella bindings used to be thought of only as racing bindings, but recreational skiers have discovered that they are also excellent for everyday touring.

Another type of binding which is still used by many is the cable binding. With this type of binding, the toe of the boot itself is not fastened to the binding. Rather, a steel cable is fitted into a groove which goes around the heel of your boot. When properly adjusted, the cable keeps your boot securely positioned in the toe piece of the binding. Cable bindings are time-proven and work well.

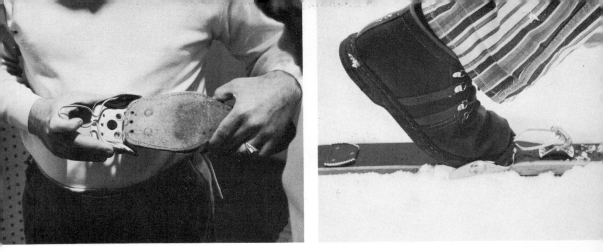

The Rottefella binding is excellent and has been used successfully for many years. It features three posts which fit into holes drilled near the toes of the ski boots. A clamp is held down by a curved toothed device. Right, the skier can lift his heel free of the ski. Lateral stability is provided by the toothed heel plate mounted to the rear of the toepiece.

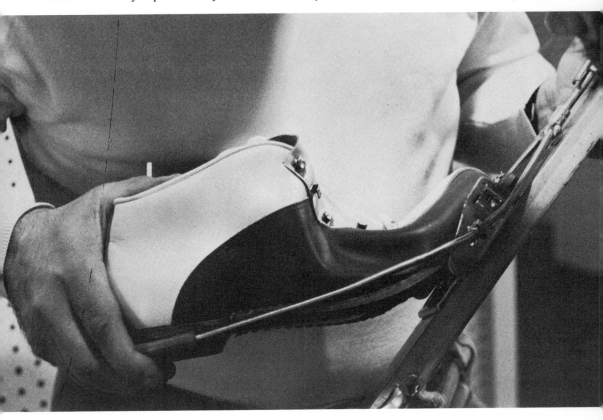

The cable binding has been used for many years by ski tourers. The toe of the ski boot fits into the toe plate and is kept there by an adjustable spring that fits into a groove around the heel of the boot. A threaded device in front of the boot toe enables skiers to adjust the cable binding to varying sizes of boots. The cable can be hooked over metal fittings at each side of the ski to provide more control when turning during a downhill run. A quick-release mechanism should be incorporated into this type of binding to avoid injury in a fall.

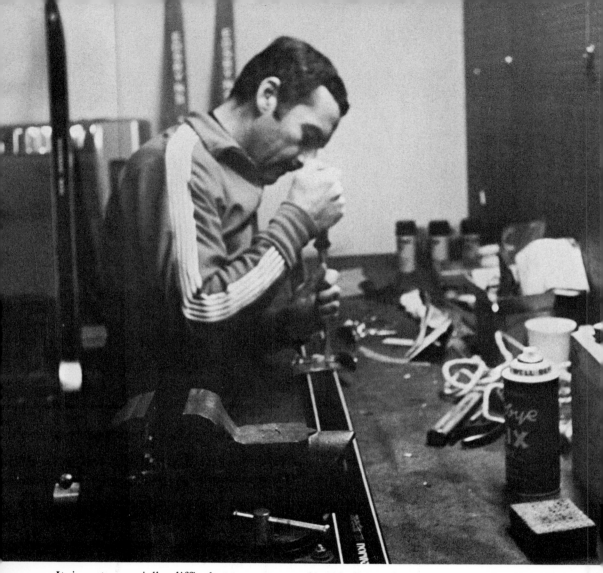

It is not especially difficult to mount touring bindings. The trick is in getting them mounted on the right spot, and it is better to leave this job to an expert.

However, many tourers feel that they get much more freedom and flexibility with bindings that do away completely with the cable and simply fasten the toes of their boots to their skis.

The professional who sells you your equipment will recommend a good binding which will be suitable for your purpose.

Bindings must be installed at just the right spot on your skis. For this reason, it is better to have them mounted at the ski shop, rather than to try to do the job yourself.

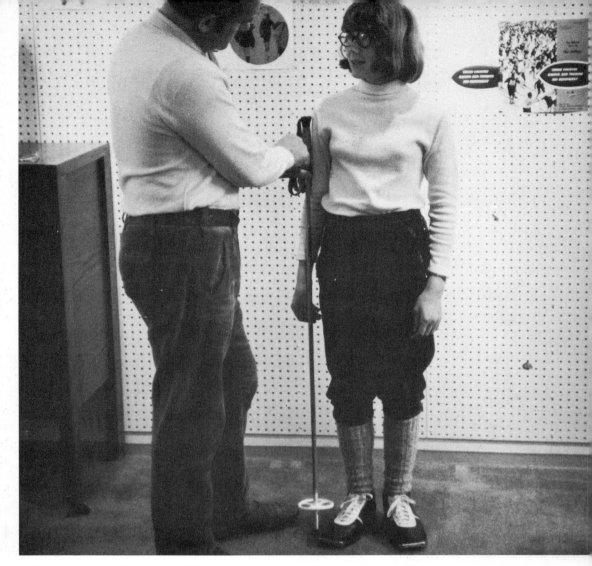

It is easy to select poles of the right length: stand up straight and place the pole next to you. If the top of the pole reaches halfway between your armpit and your shoulder, it is the right length.

Poles: Ski touring poles are made of bamboo, and are light, strong, and springy. At the upper end there is a handle and a strap. At the lower end there is a curved steel tip and, just above it, a round ring called a basket. The basket prevents the pole from sinking too deeply into the snow when it is used. The tip is curved to make it easy for you to pull your pole out of the snow after you have skied past it.

To choose poles of the right length, stand up straight. A touring pole, when placed beside you, should reach halfway between your armpit and the top of your shoulder, as shown in the photo.

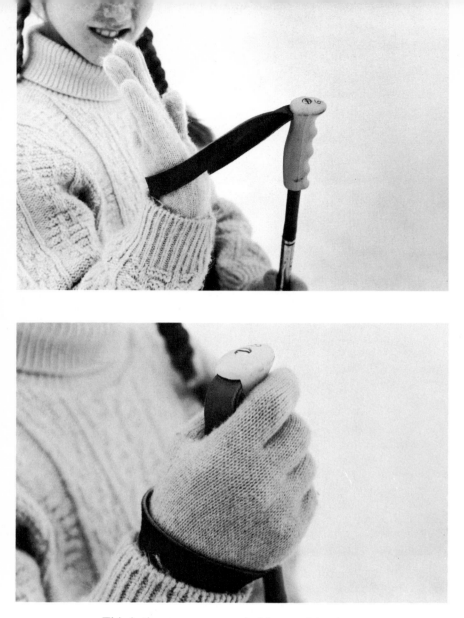

This is the proper way to hold your ski poles.

The strap at the top of the pole is there to help you hang onto the pole while skiing. As shown in the photos, open the strap, put your hand into the loop from below, then grasp the handle of the pole. The strap should fit around your hand without twisting.

Touring pole straps are longer than those on Alpine poles. Some touring poles feature straps which are adjustable in length. There are some occasions when you may want to vary the effective length of the pole. Thus, to "shorten" your pole, you simply move your hand down the shaft—a technique especially useful when climbing up a hill. To "lengthen" the pole, just place your hand near or on the top of the pole. "Long" poles are especially useful when skiing on flat terrain.

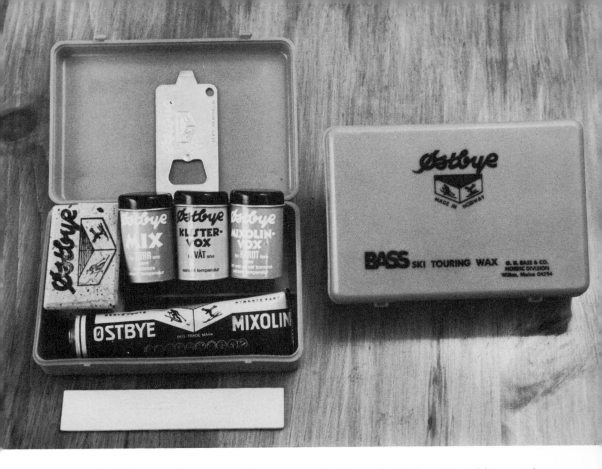

A wax kit is inexpensive and usually comes packed in a plastic box. Most kits contain a waxing cork, scraper, three hard waxes, a klister or two, and a wooden paddle for spreading the klister. The Østbye/Bass kit shown above is a good starting kit. It contains a variety of waxes necessary for most recreational touring. Note that the scraper has a bottle opener and a useful, screwdriver-like projection that can be used for tightening your binding screws.

Wax: Skis are waxed so they will grip the snow when they are motionless, and slide over the snow when you put them into motion. Unwaxed wooden or plastic ski bottoms cannot do this.

At first, waxing might seem to be a complicated business. It is not. Once you learn a few simple facts about snow conditions and how to match wax to those conditions, you will be able to pick the correct wax just about every time.

There are many different kinds of snow, ranging from very dry, light, fluffy, newly fallen powder to wet, sloppy, mushy slush. The trick is to choose the wax appropriate to the condition of the snow over which you will be skiing. Check chapter four for waxing techniques.

3 | CLOTHING

Most people keep warm while outdoors in winter simply by adding a jacket or sweater. In other words, they insulate themselves with additional clothing.

Another way to keep warm is by exercising. You will get enough exercise on a touring trip to keep you warm even though you are lightly dressed. The body heat generated by your movements and by the increased rate of blood circulation is considerable. You will be quite comfortable while wearing only two layers of thin clothing.

Knickers are preferred by many experienced skiers because they permit freedom of leg movement. They are worn with long woolen knee socks. "Helanca" is a stretch nylon fabric which has been successfully used in touring clothing. It stretches, "breathes" well, and is warm and light.

You can buy special touring clothes if you wish. However, almost any clothing that you would wear in winter will do, as long as it fits loosely and is not too heavy or bulky. If the winters are cold where you live, you probably have enough clothing to begin touring. In touring, style does not matter. But it is important for your clothing to fit comfortably and be loose enough to permit you to move freely.

Wear your clothing in thin layers. This allows you to take off a layer at a time as you get warmer during a trip—it also allows you to put on additional layers if you start to get cold. When you stop for lunch or for some other reason, put on another sweater until you get moving again.

Pants: Your pants should fit you loosely enough to allow you to move your legs freely. Knickers and woolen knee socks permit this freedom of movement. The close-fitting stretch pants worn by Alpine skiers are not very suitable for touring. They are too tight and will strain your leg muscles unnecessarily. If your trousers are made of a tightly woven material, they will keep moisture out and retain your body heat more efficiently.

Ski touring clothing should be comfortable and allow for free movement. A pair of knickers and wool knee socks are excellent. For the upper body, a couple of light sweaters, or a sweater and nylon windbreaker are usually all you will need, even in cold weather.

Long Underwear: Woolen underwear is best. It will keep you warm even if it gets wet. Cotton will not do this. Underwear should fit snugly, but not tightly.

Sweaters: While you're on the trail, two layers are usually adequate, even in cold weather. Some tourers prefer to wear a wool sweater next to their skin, over which they wear an unlined wind shirt, or nylon shell. The shell is especially useful when skiing while snow is falling. Snowflakes will not stick to nylon, as they will to a sweater.

It's a good idea to carry a spare sweater in your back pack. You can put it on when you stop for a rest, or for lunch, or even for a long downhill run. The sweater will keep you warm until you begin skiing again.

Gloves: In mild weather you may not even need gloves. Almost any winter gloves will do for touring, but the best combination is a woolen inner mitten or glove with a leather outer shell, as shown on page 27. By using the liner/shell combination, you can remove the shell if your hands get too warm, and replace it if they get cold. Either gloves or mittens may be worn, but mittens are warmer.

Hats and Head Bands: The warmest arrangement is a wool winter hat which can be pulled down over your ears. Most of the time, though, a headband will keep your ears warm enough. In mild weather, you may not need anything on your head.

Socks: A pair of winter woolen socks should be warm enough. However, in cold weather you may want to wear two pairs—a thin pair under a heavy pair.

Sunglasses: It is a good idea to bring along a pair of sunglasses, particularly if you expect to be skiing over open, unshaded fields. Sunlight reflected off the snow can be uncomfortably bright.

Back Pack: A back pack is useful for carrying such items as a spare sweater, a waxing kit, a torch, your lunch, a thermos of hot chocolate, even a spare ski tip in case someone breaks a ski.

The best packs, although the most expensive, are made of nylon. They have padded, adjustable straps. Some of them have separate pockets so you can take out and replace various items without disturbing everything in the pack.

Army surplus canvas rucksacks can also be used, although they are neither as durable nor as conveniently organized as the special ski touring back packs. They cost much less, though.

Before buying a back pack, try it on and make sure the shoulder straps and waist strap can be adjusted for proper fit.

Fanny Pack: A fanny pack is made of canvas, nylon, or leather and is strapped around your waist much like a belt. It will not carry as much as a back pack but is useful for carrying small items.

These skiers, about to enjoy a trip through the Green Mountains of Vermont, are dressed lightly and comfortably in sweaters, knickers, and woolen knee socks.

A nylon backpack is useful for containing such items as a spare sweater. You will need this sweater when you stop for lunch during a trip.

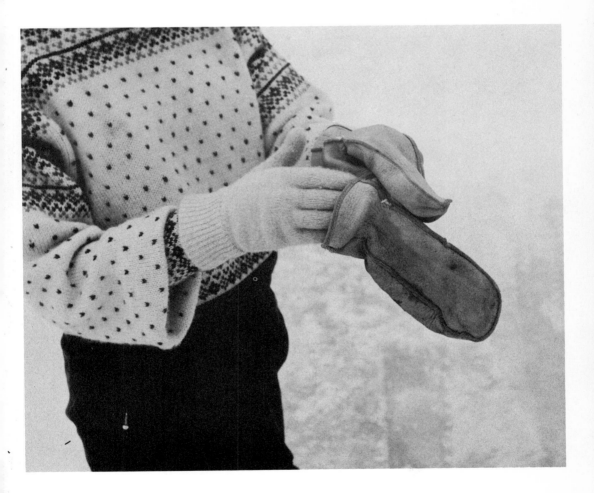

An ideal way of keeping your hands warm while touring is by wearing a woolen inner glove or mitten and a leather outer shell.

Many ski tourers find that an Army surplus rucksack is useful. This touring family has stopped for a lunch break during a trip through the woods.

4. | WAXING

Touring skis must be waxed before each trip. Alpine skis are seldom waxed, except by racers. Why does one type of ski have to be waxed but not the other?

The answer lies in the difference between Alpine skiing and touring. Alpine skiers are lifted or towed to the top of a hill, then ski more or less straight down. Thus, Alpine skis are built to go in one direction only—downhill. To make this easy, the bottoms of Alpine skis are coated with a special plastic which allows a skier to ski downhill as fast as he wishes, without waxing.

Touring skis are used for skiing uphill as well as downhill. Their bottoms must be treated with the magic stuff which makes this possible: touring wax.
Touring skis must be treated with:

1. Base preparations (pine tar or Grundvalla) which are applied over the bare wood to seal out moisture and provide a good surface to which the running waxes can grip.

2. Running waxes, those compounds which actually come into contact with the snow.

3. In some cases, with Grundvax.

How Wax Helps You Ski: Waxed skis do two very different jobs. They *grip* the snow while the ski is motionless and weighted, and they *glide* over it when the ski is set into motion. If your skis couldn't do this, it would be difficult for you to tour over the countryside.

The waxing torch

Waxes can be put on and taken off without the use of a torch. However, using a torch will make these jobs much easier.

The basic tools used in waxing: a torch, a rag, and a wax kit containing a cork, a wooden paddle for spreading klisters, a scraper, and waxes. The entire outfit is light and small and fits easily into a backpack.

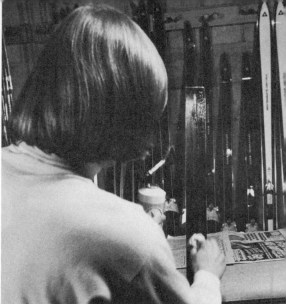

To remove wax from your skis, heat the ski bottoms with your torch and wipe off the softened wax. Work on an 8- or 12-inch section at a time.

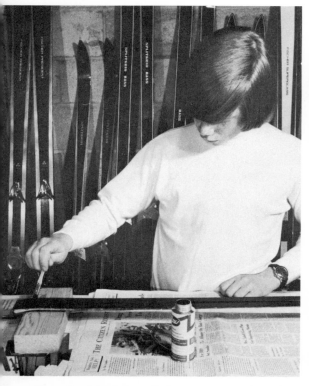

The liquid type of base preparation is painted on the ski bottoms, then torched.

Aerosol base preparation is simply sprayed on. It does not last as long as the pine tar base preparation, but it is a lot easier to apply.

A torch is used to put on base preparations and running waxes. It is also used to remove old waxes. If you and your friends are planning a touring trip of any length at all, it is a good idea to take a torch with you, in case anyone has to change waxes during the trip. The torch shown in the photos is light and small. It fits easily into a touring back pack and can be used anywhere.

When you use a torch, remember: *Keep moving.* Keep the flame moving back and forth to prevent the ski from getting burned.

You will have to use both hands when working with your torch. One hand handles the torch while the other works with a cork or a spreader or a rag. You will not be able to hold the skis, so they must be secured in a position that permits you to work on them easily. In professional ski shops, special vises are used. However, you can get by either by leaning the skis against a wall and having a friend hold them or by placing them on two by fours on a table, with plenty of newspapers under the skis to keep the wax off the table.

Base preparation

If the wooden bottoms of touring skis aren't sealed with a base preparation they will absorb water and warp out of shape. Ice will also build up on them during a trip.

Also, though running waxes will not stick to bare, untreated wood, they will stick easily to skis that have been base treated.

Types of Base Preparations: There are three kinds of base preparations:
  1) aerosol spray,
  2) liquid, applied with a cloth or paintbrush, and
  3) pine tar preparation rubbed on the skis and melted in with a torch.
The first two types are easiest to apply, but the third type lasts longest.

New Skis: Some new skis have a factory-applied protective coating on their bottoms. It is put there to prevent the skis from absorbing moisture and warping before they are used. Before you apply the base preparation, sandpaper this coating off. Other skis, such as the Splitkein/Bass, have a factory-applied base preparation that should not be removed. Be sure you ask the sales person from whom you buy your skis whether or not the bottoms should be sandpapered.

Old Skis: At the beginning of the season—and periodically during the season (depending on how often you go skiing)—the base preparation wll have to be replaced. Scrape off excess waxes. Light up your waxing torch and pass it back and forth over the ski bottoms until the wax has softened. Wipe off the heated wax with a cloth. Continue until all the old wax has been removed. Before you apply a new coat of base preparation, look over your skis carefully. Smooth out any bumps or irregularities with sandpaper or steel wool before you recondition them.

How to Apply Base Preparation: When the aerosol type of base preparation is used, the torch is not needed. This type of preparation will penetrate the ski's running surface without having to be heated.

If you use the liquid or pine tar preparation, you will find them easier to apply if you use a torch to help you. Spread a thin layer of the base preparation on your ski bottoms, including the groove. Pass your torch over the bottoms, an 8- to 10-inch section at a time, to melt the preparation into the pores of the wood. Wipe off the excess preparation with a rag.

Press your finger against the ski bottom. If it is just a little sticky, the base preparation was properly applied. It would be a mistake to put the preparation on too thickly. A thin, barely sticky coating is just right.

You can go ahead and apply the running wax now—unless conditions call for the application of a binder (called Grundvax).

Binding wax (Grundvax)—what it is:

Grundvax is a specialty compound which is quite useful if the snow is very crusty and likely to wear the ski bottoms. Should you be using touring skis which have plastic bottoms, Grundvax will help the running wax to stick to the plastic. Most of the time, though, Grundvax will not be required.

To apply, just rub it on the ski. Either rub it in with a waxing cork or use the torch to soften it, then smooth it in with the cork. When it is properly rubbed in, it will be almost impossible to see.

Running waxes

Because running wax permits your skis to alternately grip the snow and glide over it, you can ski anywhere you can find a snow-covered surface. When your skis are properly waxed, you should be able to climb straight up an incline without sliding back. You will also be able to slide easily down the other side of the hill, if you wish.

Running waxes are divided into hard waxes and klister, or semi-liquid waxes. Hard waxes vary in consistency from that of an ordinary wax candle to soft and very sticky. They come in small tins made of heavy aluminum or lead foil. The klisters are *very* sticky and gooey. They come in a toothpaste-type tube. Make certain you put the cap on after each use. If you don't, the klister will ooze out and make things pretty messy.

Why There Are Different Kinds of Waxes: No one has yet invented an all-purpose wax, one which will work well on all kinds of snow. Until that day comes, when we go touring we must find out what kind of snow we will be skiing over, then put on the appropriate wax.

Snow can be light, dry, fluffy, and powdery; or wet, sticky, and heavy; or icy, crusty, and lumpy. There are many other variations of snow. Also, snow conditions change from day to day—even from hour to hour. Conditions can also change from place to place during the same trip. The snow will be wetter and stickier in the sunny, unshaded open fields than it will in the woods, where it is shaded by trees.

The wax which works well on dry powder snow will not be at all suitable for skiing over wet, sticky snow. These two different types of snow present two quite different surfaces on which your skis must alternately grip and glide.

Thus, as snow conditions change, the kind of wax you should use will also change. It is easy, though, to figure out which kind of wax to use. The instructions in this book and on the wax tins and tubes can help you to make the correct choice each time. Also, a bit of practice is needed before the correct choice becomes second nature.

Which Brand of Wax to Use: There are several brands of touring wax now on the market. They are all good. The important thing is not so much which brand you use as it is that you pick one brand and stick with it—at least until you become used to its special characteristics. Later you can experiment with other brands if you wish.

Another reason for not switching brands at first is that each brand has its own color-coded system. The different waxes are identified by the color of the tin or tube in which they are packed, and these colors are not standardized. For example, snow conditions which call for you to use violet Rex wax would require the use of red Swix wax, or the yellow Østbye wax.

If you were a cross-country ski racer, it would be necessary for you to pick the wax which would be exactly right for the snow conditions during a race. There are many, many different kinds of waxes—and they can be used in dozens of combinations. Racers are familiar with these different combinations and know how to use the different waxes to get the very highest speeds over a race course. To them, applying precisely the right wax is one of the most important things they can do, apart from actually running the race.

Since your reason for skiing is simply to have fun, you can simplify your waxing by narrowing your choices to a few which will work well over a fairly wide range of snow conditions. For you, it isn't important that you apply exactly the proper wax to get the most speed. That is why you will find simplified waxing procedures in this book. The whole idea is to get you out onto the snow-covered trails and fields so you can begin to enjoy yourself as soon as possible. If, later, you become interested in learning the magic formulae used by racers, you can.

It was with this in mind that Østbye waxes were chosen for the photos in this book. The Østbye wax kits contain just four waxes—and they are adequate for most snow conditions. The kit comes in a plastic box together with a cork, scraper, and a wooden stick for spreading the klister. The kit is small enough to be carried easily in your back pack, just in case you have to rewax while out on a trip.

Before You Wax: Make sure the ski bottoms are dry and that old running waxes

The longest lasting base preparation is made from pine tar. It is brushed on, as shown here, then torched.

Hard waxes come in soft foil tubes. Peel off the top quarter inch, as shown, to expose the candlelike hard wax.

have been removed. Most waxing is done indoors; however, some skiers prefer to apply hard waxes outside.

Matching Wax to Snow Conditions

Always wax for the driest, coldest conditions you think you will encounter. You can always put a softer wax on top of the wax already on your skis, but you cannot apply a harder wax over one which is softer. Remember: *Wax hard.*

Generally, the hardest tube waxes are used for skiing over dry, powdery snow and the sticky klisters are used to ski over wet, sloppy slush. The waxes in between are used for in-between snow conditions.

The three hard waxes and Mixolin klister are packaged in the Østbye waxing kit mentioned in this chapter. With this kit, you can prepare your skis for most conditions you will encounter and you can expect good enough results for recreational skiing.

Following is a general description of which Østbye waxes to apply according to snow conditions:

Dry, Powdery Snow: Use Østbye Mix, in the blue tin. Make sure it is applied evenly, and not too thickly. This hard wax can be applied outdoors, where it is cold, but it is much easier to apply indoors, to a warmed ski. If you wax your skis with blue Mix and try them out, only to find they don't grip as they should, you can always add a coat of Mixolin, in the orange tin, over the blue. The orange is softer and will give you better results if the snow should have a higher moisture content than you had originally thought and, depending on the temperature, this could be either soft or hard snow.

Wet, Granular Snow: Use Østbye Klister Vox, in the yellow tin, for snow with a very high moisture content—either snow you can squeeze moisture from or icy snow. Usually this is used when the temperature is well above freezing. The wetter the snow, the thicker should be the coat of wax you apply, particularly in the center sections of the ski bottoms. For snow which is moist, but not wet, use orange wax.

Old, Crusty Snow: Use Østbye Mixolin Vox, in the orange tin. Whether the surface is dry, or wet, or hard, this wax will work well if you're planning a trip over old snow which has been repeatedly frozen and thawed, but which is not icy.

Spring Skiing Conditions: Much of the time when the temperature is above freezing, the snow will be sloppy enough to require a klister. There are several klisters available, but the one which comes closest to being an all-pupose klister is Østbye Mixolin, in the blue and yellow tube. For most occasions, you can apply this klister and get pretty good results.

Hard wax should be applied as a thin coating. Just rub it on, as shown.

The soft tube waxes are quite sticky and can best be applied by rolling the exposed portion of the wax along the ski.

To apply klister, squeeze it out of the tube in a ribbonlike strip, as shown.

Klister should be spread with a scraper or a wooden paddle. Smooth it out so it covers your ski bottoms. Be careful not to get any klister in the grooves.

How to Judge Snow Conditions: Scoop up a handful. Squeeze it as you would when making a snowball. Open your hand. If the snowball falls apart, the snow is dry; if it keeps its shape, it is moist; and if you have squeezed water out of the snowball, the snow is wet. Other kinds of snow are hard and crusty or wet, sloppy, and slushy.

How to Apply Waxes

Apply Hard Tube Waxes: Remove the top and peel off about 1/4 inch of the tin, as shown in the photo. Rub the wax along the entire length of both ski bottoms in a thin layer. Some skiers use a torch at this point to melt the wax before rubbing it in. Others believe that hard waxes should be rubbed in with a cork, but need not be torched. If you use a torch, run the flame back and forth along the ski in sections of 8 to 10 inches. Working section by section, apply just enough heat to melt the wax, not burn it. Rub the wax smooth with your waxing cork. When both skis are waxed, put them outside in the cold for about ten minutes before you use them, if you waxed indoors. If you use them immediately after removing them from a warm room, ice will form on their bottoms.

Apply Soft Tube Waxes: Some of the so-called hard waxes are pretty soft and sticky, even though they come in a tin. After you tear off the top 1/4 inch of the tin, apply the wax by rolling the exposed wax along the ski bottom, as shown in the photo on page 36. Then, rub it with your cork as you would a harder wax.

Apply Klister Waxes: Squeeze the klister out slowly as you move the tube along each side of the ski bottom. Use a wooden paddle or a scraper to spread the klister over the surface of the ski bottom. Then, use your torch to melt the wax. You can use either a paintbrush or a scraper to spread the wax.

Keep klister out of the groove. You can rub a cake of ordinary paraffin wax along the groove to keep the klister from sticking. If klister gets into the groove, snow and ice will collect. This will slow you down.

Try Out Your Waxed Skis: Even though you're sure you've made just the right choice of wax, it makes sense to try out your skis. Ski for 200 to 300 yards with your waxed skis, just to test your wax. If you remember to wax for the coldest conditions you might encounter, it will be easy to put on a softer wax—if that should be necessary. If you have applied a wax which is too hard for the snow conditions, they won't grip the snow. You will slide backward when trying to ski up a hill, for example. If your wax is too soft for conditions, you won't be able to slide downhill as well as you should.

5 | GETTING
STARTED
ON
SKIS

Touring techniques are easy to learn, since the basic touring step is similar to walking. For your first couple of sessions on skis, pick a flat spot rather than a hillside. This allows you to concentrate on learning the basics without worrying about sliding downhill. Later, you can work out on a hill. Your backyard will do fine if it is flat, otherwise you can use a snow-covered field, woods, road, golf course, or other such area.

Although touring is easy, be prepared to fall once in a while. Everyone—whether novice or expert—falls occasionally. Have patience with yourself. If you have a relaxed and happy attitude, an occasional fall won't bother you.

Touring can be enjoyed just about anywhere by skiers of all ages. Techniques are easy to learn and equipment is inexpensive. After a short session of instruction, the whole outdoors is yours to explore.

It is no disgrace to fall—everyone
does it.

Wax your skis according to the directions in chapter four. Put them on as
shown in the photographs.

1

2

3

4

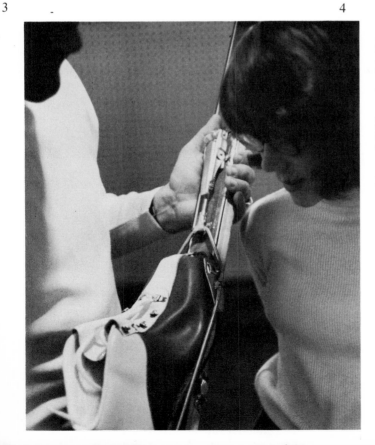

Putting on your skis. (1) If you use Rottefella bindings, place your toe in the toe plate of the binding and, (2) secure it to the ski. If you use Eie/Bass bindings, line up the toe of your boot with the binding, (3) and click your boot into the binding, (4). If you use cable bindings, place the toe of your boot into the toepiece, place the cable around the heel groove in your boot, and fasten the boot to the ski by using the front throw unit, (5).

Walking on Skis: The photographs show the best way of walking on skis. Remember to keep your back straight, your knees slightly bent, and your weight evenly distributed between your heels and the balls of your feet. Keep your skis on the surface of the snow as you slide along—don't lift them up with each step. Keep your skis from six to eight inches apart, depending on your size.

Practice walking back and forth in a straight line. Use your poles to help push you along. See how far you can glide forward with each step. If you have applied the proper wax for the snow over which you are skiing, you will be able to glide on first one ski, then the other. Why? Because the wax grips the snow when you push off and allows your skis to slide when set into motion.

Perhaps you will notice as you walk and glide along that your weight shifts from one ski to the other. You might also notice that it is the ski with your weight on it—the *weighted* ski—that glides. We will use the terms *weighted* and *unweighted* in this book to describe techniques of moving over the snow.

The walking/gliding stride is a little like ice skating or roller skating. The motions are: push off, slide—push off, slide, and your weight shifts from one ski to the other, which is similar to what happens in skating. Unlike skating, however, the direction in which you point your skis is directly forward—not to one side.

Your poles are of great assistance in helping you to learn touring. They will help you to keep your balance and they can help you go farther with each gliding step. The most natural method of poling is diagonally. For instance, as you prepare to kick with your left foot, you stick your right pole into the snow (the term for this is "planting your pole") about as far forward as your left foot. You actually kick off with the left ski and push with your right pole. As you glide past your planted pole, your poling arm gradually straightens out and you bring your other arm forward, ready to plant the opposite pole.

Notice that the skier in the photo doesn't look down at his skis. He keeps his head up so he can look ahead. Get into this habit of looking forward. It is less tiring than looking down at your skis. You will also find the habit of looking forward useful when you are picking a course through the woods or on a downhill run.

Walking on skis is easy. Keep your back straight, your knees slightly bent, and your weight evenly distributed over the center of the skis. Slide one ski forward, (1), and push with the opposite pole; bring the other ski forward and again push off with the opposite pole, (2). Repeat the process, (3), and you'll be gliding along like an expert in no time.

Keep your skis pointed straight ahead. The skier left is attempting to ski along on flat terrain with the tails of her skis spread. This is a mistake. She can go no faster than she can walk since it is impossible to glide in a straight line if her skis are not pointed straight ahead.

The Step Turn: This is a way of turning around while standing in one spot. It is not a running turn, which would be done while you're in motion. The photos and captions show you how the step turn is done.

The step turn is easy. As shown, simply take small steps in the direction in which you want to turn.

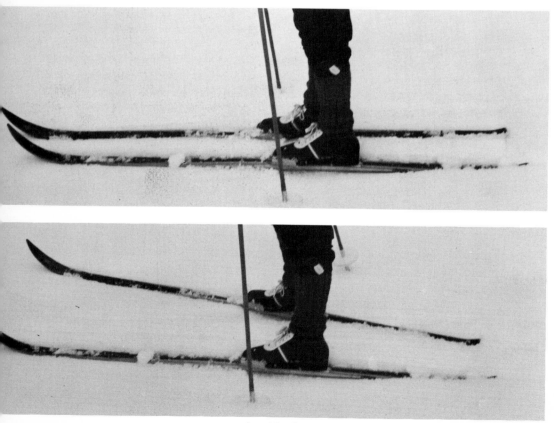

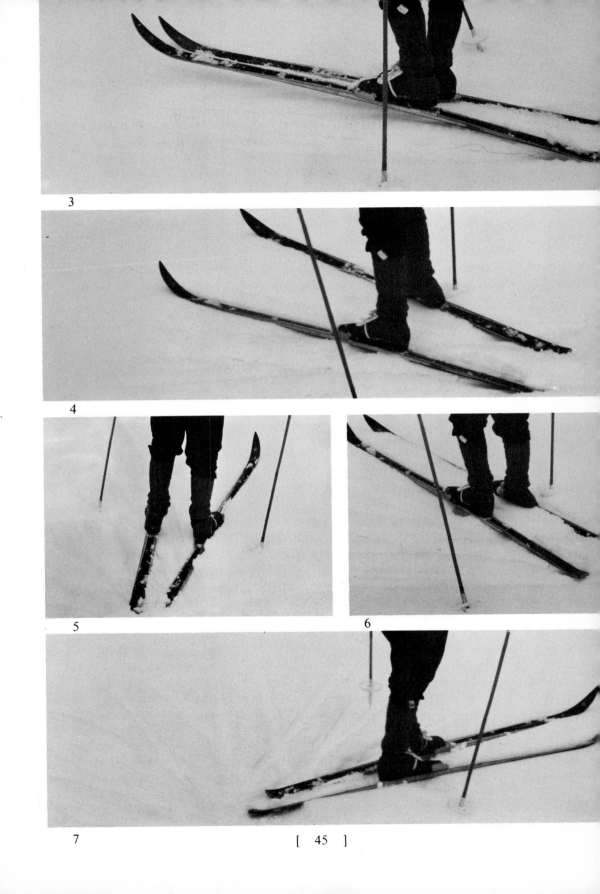

3

4

5

6

The Kick Turn: This is also a standing-in-one-place turn. It can be used either on a flat spot or on a hill. The captions and photos show you how.

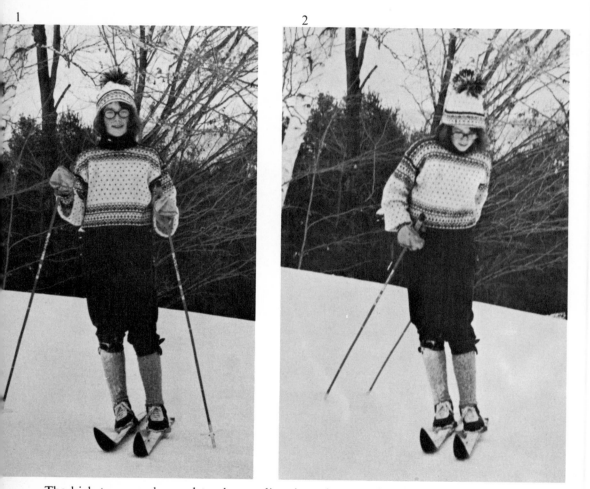

1   2

The kick turn can be used to change direction when standing in one place, either on a hill or on a flat spot. (1) keep your knees slightly bent. If you are standing on a hillside, "edge" your skis by pushing your ankles and knees toward the hill. The skier above has her uphill ski edged, her downhill ski flat on the snow, and is likely to slide downhill. (2) Place the baskets of your poles uphill from you. Note that both her skis are now edged into the hill. (3) Leaning against your poles, swing your downhill ski, tip up, around as shown above. (4) Place the downhill ski so that it points straight across the hill. If you are on a hill, edge in your ski to keep it from sliding downhill. (5) Swing your other ski and pole around. (6) The turn is complete and the skier is facing in the opposite direction.

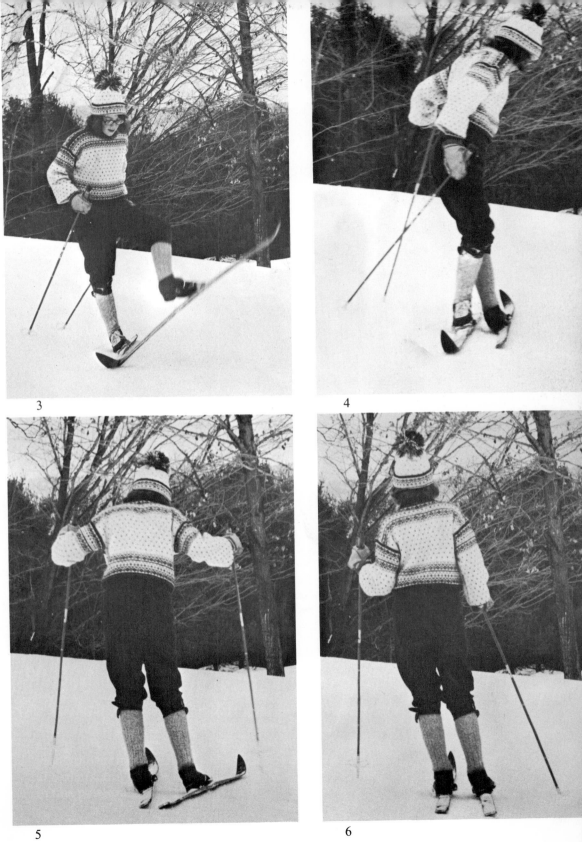

3

4

5

6

1

2

3

When you fall on flat terrain, make sure that you keep your poles away from your body, as shown here, in (1). (2) Bring your skis together, and use your poles to help you to stand up. (3) This skier is now ready to resume her trip.

How to Get Up From a Fall: Serious accidents are rare in ski touring because only the toe of your boot is fastened to your ski and because speeds are low. When you fall, your skis can move freely because they are not rigidly attached to your ski boots. As a result, there is usually very little or no torque or twisting of your legs and a fall represents nothing more than a temporary interruption of your ski trip.

Getting Up on Flat Terrain: Place your skis a few inches apart, and pointing in the same direction, and simply stand up. You might want the help of your poles. The photos and captions show you how to get up.

Getting Up On a Hillside: Swing your legs and skis around so that your skis are pointed across the hill and are pointed neither up nor downhill. Put both poles together, on the uphill side of your body, as shown in the photo. Push against your poles, and raise yourself to a standing position. Brush the snow off your clothes, adjust your skis and poles , if necessary, and resume your skiing.

1

2   3

When you fall on a hillside, (1) swing your skis around so that they are downhill from you and pointed straight across the hill, neither up- nor downhill. (2) Bring both ski poles together, place the tips in the snow, and push against the poles to help you stand up. (3) Stand up. Put your hands back in your pole straps, and resume skiing. Note that the skier above has edged her skis in so that she will not slide sideways down the hill.

1

2

3

4

When you fall in deep powder, bring your skis around so that they are together and pointed in the same direction. (1) If you are on a hillside, as shown here, make sure that your skis are placed across the hill so that they are pointed neither uphill nor downhill, and edge in your skis to keep from sliding sideways down the slope. (2) Make an X with your ski poles, uphill from you. (3) Push against your ski poles—where they cross—to help you stand up. (4) Brush off the snow, put on your pole straps, and resume your skiing.

Getting Up in Deep Powder: In the instructions above, on getting up on a hillside, you were told to keep your two poles together, uphill from your body, and use them to push yourself to a standing position. However, this will not work in deep powder since your poles would just sink into the fluffy stuff. In deep powder, make an X with your two poles, as shown in the photo. Place your hand in the center of the X, where the poles cross and push yourself up. The crossed poles distribute your weight along their length, which helps to keep them from sinking into the powder. When you fall on a hill in deep powder, bring your two crossed poles uphill from your body.

Putting It Together

With just a little practice, you will be able to walk and glide along on a level spot and make a kick turn and a step turn. You will also be able to get up after a fall. Before you begin learning to ski up and down hills, practice these maneuvers until you can do them easily, almost automatically.

Practice on a level snow-covered area of some size, such as a field or wide trail. Keep walking and gliding in a straight line until you come to the edge of your practice area. Make a kick turn and kick/glide back toward your starting point, using the tracks you made during your first trip. When you again come to the edge of the practice area, make a step turn and retrace your tracks.

As you go back and forth, try to glide farther and farther with each step. You will be able to go faster and glide farther if you use your poles. Correct use of the poles is almost instinctive, but, for the record, use, or plant, them diagonally. That is, as you glide forward on your left ski, you stick your right pole in the snow (or "plant" it) and push with it. Plant your left pole and push with it as you glide on your right ski. In other words, the pole opposite the weighted, gliding ski is used to push you along.

After a few trips back and forth on this ski track, try skiing in circles and squares. This helps you to learn the skating turn. The skating turn is just a common-sense way of changing direction when skiing on fairly flat terrain. It can be used also on downhill runs, especially when the slope isn't too steep.

The Skating Turn: This is an easy-to-learn method of changing direction while remaining in motion. It is such a natural technique that, if someone else hadn't already thought of it, you probably would. It consists of changing direction gradually by stepping your skis, a few degrees at a time, toward the new direction in which you want to travel.

For illustration, let's assume you are skiing along at a good clip on flat terrain and want to turn to the left. As you weight your right ski, lift the left ski off the snow and point it in a direction to the left of your original direction. Weight it and bring your right ski around so it is parallel to—and a few inches away from—your left ski. Simply repeat this process until you are headed in the new direction of travel. To turn to the right, point the right ski to the right of the original direction of travel until you're headed in the new direction.

6 SKIING UP AND DOWN A GENTLE HILL

After you have learned to walk and glide along on skis on a level surface and after you have learned the step turn, the kick turn, and the skating turn, you will be ready to learn to ski up and down hill.

HOW TO SKI UPHILL

You can ski straight up a hill—as long as it isn't *too* steep—or you can climb up. To climb, you can use either the side step or the herringbone.

Edging In: If, when you are standing sideways on a hill, your skis are flat on the snow, chances are they will slide downhill. To prevent this from occurring, you can push your knees and ankles toward the hill. When you do this, the uphill edges of your skis dig into, or edge into, the snow. When the term "edge in" is used in this book, remember to push your knees and ankles toward the hill so the edges of your skis can get a grip on the surface of the snow.

Skiing Straight Up a Hill: The best body position to use when you ski straight up a hill is achieved by squatting slightly, as if you were about to sit down in a chair. Keep your back fairly straight and your chin up, so you can look up the slope. Keep your weight evenly balanced between the balls of your feet and your heels. This distributes your body weight evenly along the lengths of your skis, which

You will find it easier to ski uphill if you remember to bend your knees, keep your weight centered and evenly divided on your skis, and the baskets of your poles behind you.

A common error made by beginners is to lean forward while walking straight up a hill. If you do this, your weight will be concentrated toward the tips, and your ski wax will not be able to grip the snow.

permits the maximum possible amount of wax to come into contact with, and grip, the snow.

Do not lean forward. If you do, your weight will be concentrated on the forward part of your skis and the wax can't grip the snow efficiently.

Assume this beginning-squat position and just begin walking uphill. Keep your skis a comfortable distance apart and pointed straight up the slope. Pole diagonally as you would when walking on a level surface.

This skier is walking up a slight hill and is bringing her left pole forward to help her progress.

1

2

3

4

The side step is used when climbing steep hills. It might help if you pretend that you are climbing an imaginary set of stairs. To do this, and to keep your ski flat on the "stair" with each step, you will have to edge your skis at an angle to the surface of the snow. (1) Keep your knees slightly bent and support yourself, if necessary, with your poles. (2) Move your uphill ski and pole up the slope a few inches. (3) Bring your downhill ski and pole uphill, as shown. (4) Repeat the process with your uphill ski. (5) Again, bring your downhill ski up the slope. Repeat this process until you climb as high as desired.

5

The Side Step: When climbing steep hills, the side step can be used.

1. Stand at the base of the hill with your skis parallel, a few inches apart, and pointed across the hill, neither up nor down the slope. Keep your knees and ankles pushed in toward the hill so that your skis are edged in.

2. Move your uphill ski and pole a foot or so up the slope. Stamp down with your ski and edge it in. This will pack the snow and reduce the chances of sliding downhill, sideways. The distance you cover with each step will depend on your size and, to some extent, the steepness of the hill.

3. Bring your downhill ski and pole the same distance up the slope.

4. Continue up the slope, moving your skis and poles together and stamping your skis down and edging in with each step.

Should you want to side step up a hill and, at the same time, ski across the face of it, just slide your skis forward with each step you take up the slope. The photos show how the side step traverse is done.

1   2

The side step traverse is used when you want to climb a hill and at the same time move diagonally across the slope. (1) As this skier moves her uphill ski up the slope, she also slides it forward a few inches. (2) She has brought her downhill ski up and across the slope so that it is even with her uphill ski, and is prepared once again to slide her uphill ski up the slope and forward.

1

The herringbone is a faster way of skiing uphill than the side step. However, it is a more tiring method and is generally used for short distances. Spread your tips so

The Herringbone: This step provides a much faster way of climbing than the side step. It is also more tiring and is used most often on short, steep hills.

1. Stand at the base of a gentle hill. Slide the tips of your skis apart so they form a V.
2. Push your knees toward each other so that the inside edges of your skis are edged into the snow.
3. Start walking straight up the slope, remembering to keep your ski tips spread apart and your knees pushed toward each other. Lift your skis off the snow and stamp them down with each step.
4. Use your poles to help push you up the hill. Plant them in the snow a little

that they form a V. Push your knees together to let the inside edges of your skis bite into the snow. Support yourself with your poles. (1) Take a step uphill a comfortable distance with your left ski. (2) Bring your right ski uphill as shown. Continue this process until you have climbed as high as desired.

farther behind you (downhill) than you would when skiing on flat terrain.
5. When you tackle steeper hills you may find climbing easier if you spread the ski tips even farther apart and edge in your inside edges even more.

SKIING DOWNHILL

The best practice area to use for your first few trips downhill is a gentle hill, well covered with snow, with a flat spot or a slight upturn at the bottom of the

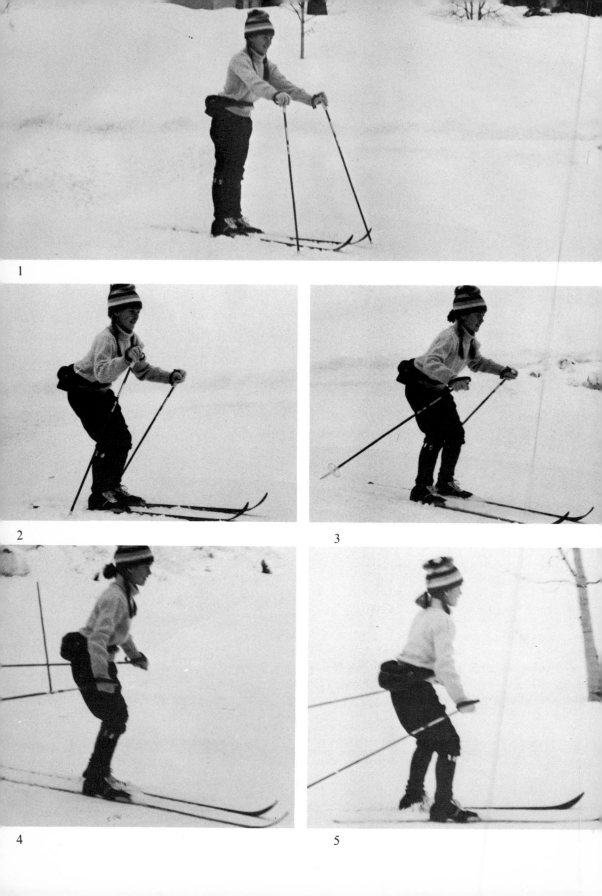

1

2

3

4

5

6

7

8

9

For your first downhill run, choose a gentle hill which has a flat area at the bottom or an upturn so you will not have to worry about stopping. (1) Stand with your skis a few inches apart and pointing in the same direction. Place your poles to keep from sliding downhill until you are ready. (2) Bend your knees and push off with your poles. (3) Keep your weight centered and evenly divided between your skis. Look ahead, not down at your skis. (4) Keep the baskets of your poles uphill from you and a few inches off the snow. (5 through 10) Remain in this position until you come to a stop. Then climb back up the hill and try another run. Stay on this gentle hill until you feel secure and ready for more challenging terrain.

slope. If you can find a hill like this, you will not have to worry about how to stop after each run, and you can concentrate first on learning to ski downhill and to make turns, and *then* learn how to stop when you want to. The following are instructions for straight downhill running.

1. Climb to the top of the practice hill.
2. Stand at the top and point your skis down the slope. Keep them about six inches apart and parallel.
3. Bend your knees slightly so they are over the toes of your boots.
4. Keep your weight centered between the balls of your feet and your heels. That is, do not lean forward or backward. Keep an equal amount of weight on each ski.
5. Keep your chin up and your eyes looking down the slope, not down at your skis.
6. Move your skis back and forth a few times to make sure snow or ice isn't sticking to their bottoms.
7. Push off with your poles. Keep your knees bent as described in 3. Hold your pole handles outward from your body and slightly in front. The baskets should be behind you and just off the surface of the snow.
8. Ski down the hill until you stop.
9. Repeat this until you can ski up and down the practice hill with no difficulty.

The Snowplow:

1. Climb to the top of the practice slope.
2. Stand at the top with your skis pointed toward the bottom.
3. Spread the tails of the skis apart, as shown in the photos, keeping the tips about six inches apart. Keep an equal amount of weight on each ski.
4. Push off with your poles to begin snowplowing down the practice slope. You will be traveling downhill a lot more slowly than you were on your straight downhill runs. The reason is that your skis offer more resistance to the snow in the snowplow position than in the parallel position.
5. You can regulate your speed during a snow plow run by varying the distance between the tails of your skis. The closer together they are, the faster you will go. The farther apart they are, the more slowly you will go. Remember to keep your ski tips about six inches apart, regardless of the distance between the tails. Try making a couple of runs with the tails close together and a couple more with the tails farther apart.
6. You can also regulate your speed by varying the amount of edging in. That is, the more you push your knees and ankles toward each other, the more the inside edges of your skis will dig into the snow, and the more resistance they will offer. The flatter your skis are on the surface of the snow, the faster you will go.
7. When you come to the bottom of the practice hill, try a snowplow stop. Push your knees and ankles together sharply to cause your skis to edge in.

1

When you snowplow down a hill, you can regulate your speed by the distance between the tails of your skis. In photo (1), above, the tails of her skis are close together and allow her to move faster than they will in photo (2) on the following page.

2

Here the tails of her skis are farther apart and will slow her down.

The Snowplow Turn: All skiing turns that are made while the skier is in motion are based on the fact that the weighted ski is the turning ski. Snowplow turns are no exception. Until now, both in running downhill and in snowplowing downhill, you have kept your weight evenly distributed between your two skis. The result is that you have skied more or less straight down the slope. If, however, you put more weight on one ski than on the other, the ski with the most weight on it will turn in the direction in which it is pointed.

1. Climb to the top of the practice hill.

Skiing turns are based on the fact that the ski that has the most weight on it will turn in the direction in which it is pointed. This skier is turning to her right because she has shifted her weight to her left ski. She could make a sharper turn if she were to edge in her left ski, and push her left knee toward the direction of her turn.

1

2

3

The Stem turn. (1) The skier is skiing diagonally down the hill. Her skis are parallel. (2) She has stemmed out with her left ski and is shifting her weight to that ski. (3) She is turning to the right since that is the direction toward which her left ski is pointed. As long as she keeps her weight on the left ski, she will continue to turn. If she wanted to come to a halt, she would simply continue her turn until her skis were pointed straight across the slope.

2. Form a snowplow with your skis and push off down the slope.

3. When you begin to pick up a little speed, rotate your shoulders to the left, lean over your left ski, and bend your left knee slightly. By leaning over to the left, you have shifted most of your weight to your left ski. Your left ski is pointed to the right, since the tips are together and the tails are apart. Because the weighted ski turns in the direction in which it is pointed, your left ski will begin a turn to the right.

4. When you feel yourself starting to turn to the right, rotate your shoulders back again so they are pointed straight ahead and reshift your weight evenly between the two skis. You will stop turning.

5. Now, rotate your shoulders to the right, lean over your right ski, and bend your right knee slightly. Because your right ski is now the weighted ski and because it is pointed to the left, you will begin turning to the left.

Practice making a series of turns to the left and the right as you snowplow down the hill, until you can make turns when and where you wish.

The Snowplow Stop: This is used when you want to stop part of the way down a hill.

1. Climb back to the top of the practice hill.

2. Get into position for snowplowing downhill.

3. Push off. As you begin to gain speed, make a turn to the right by shifting your weight to your left ski.

4. This time, instead of making a series of left/right turns, continue turning to the right. To make a quicker, or more pronounced, turn, push your downhill (left) knee toward the hill. This will edge in your turning (left) ski.

5. You will eventually stop. Why? Because if you continue the turn long enough your skis will end up pointing more or less across the slope.

6. Next, practice a snowplow stop while turning to the left.

The Stem Turn: This turn can be made while you are running straight downhill.

1. Climb to the top of the practice hill.

2. Point your skis down the hill, as you would when beginning a downhill run.

3. Push off with your poles, and begin your straight downhill run.

4. As you pick up speed, move the tail of your left ski out to form half a snowplow V ("stemming" is the term used to describe this action). At the same time, rotate your shoulders to the left and bend your left knee a little more deeply.

5. Your left ski will begin turning to the right.

6. Push your left knee and ankle into the hill. That is, toward your other knee. This permits the uphill edge of your turning (left) ski to edge into the snow, which makes turning easier.

7. When your turn has been started, slowly slide your uphill (right) ski down to within a few inches of your turning (left) ski. The two skis should now be pointed

1 2 3

in the same direction and parallel. Keep slightly more weight on your downhill (left) ski than on the other one.

8. Now, practice making a turn to the left, stemming with your right ski and rotating your shoulders to the right, and shifting your weight to the right ski.

The Step, or Skating, Turn While Skiing Downhill: The skating turn was described at the end of chapter five as a way of changing direction while skiing on flat terrain. The same method of turning can be used while you're skiing down a hill. Make sure your weight is centered between your heels and the balls of your feet. As you pick up speed on a downhill run, swing the tip of your right ski to the right so that it is pointed to the right of your original direction of travel (the direction in which your left ski is pointed). At the same time, support yourself by a slight push with your left pole. Next, lift your left ski and swing it around so that the two skis are parallel. Now, take another small step to the right with the right ski. Again, bring the left ski around so the two skis are once again parallel. Continue this until your turn to the right has been completed. Next, practice a turn to the left.

4

5

The skating turn is another way of changing direction while you are skiing down a hill. (1) This skier is moving diagonally across the face of the hill in the standard running position. Her knees are bent and her skis are parallel. (2) She has taken a step to her left with her left ski. (3) She has brought her right ski around so that it is parallel with her left ski. (4) She has taken another step to the left with her left ski. (5) She has brought her right ski around so that it is again parallel with her left ski and she is now pointed in the direction in which she wants to go.

It is important that you learn to turn in order to change direction as well as to control your downhill speed. Skiing around poles is excellent practice. (1) Plant several ski poles in a line down a gentle hill, and ski around each one. (2) This skier is turning around one pole in the sequence, and controls her speed by spreading the tails of her skis. The tips of her skis should be together a little more closely than they are in this photo.

GAMES YOU CAN PLAY

After you have practiced making downhill runs and turns, you might like to improve your skills with some easy-to-do exercises.

Skiing Around Poles: Place your ski poles and the poles of your friends in a line from the top to the bottom of your practice hill as shown in the photos. The object is to ski around each of the poles without running into them and without missing any. This is a good exercise for practicing snowplow turns and stem turns. The photos on this page show how this exercise is done.

1

Picking Up Gloves and Scarves: Scatter mittens, scarves, and other objects in a line from the top to the bottom of the practice hill. The object is to collect all the objects in one trip down the hill. This exercise is useful for developing balance and the habit of bending your knees. It will be especially helpful if you will crouch down to pick up the objects, then stand up until you approach the next object. If you want to make the exercise more difficult, scatter the items all over the face of the hill, so that you will have to make a number of sharp turns during your downhill descent. The photographs show how to do this.

2

3

A variation on the "skiing around the poles" exercise is picking up gloves, mittens, and other objects scattered down the face of a gentle hill. This exercise will develop your ability to make turns, control your speed, gain balance and flex your knees. (1) Some ski gloves and scarves have been scattered down the small hill and the skier is picking up each one in its turn. (2) She has a handful of mittens and is just about to pick up the last one. (3) Success!

Skiing Under A Bridge: This exercise will help you to become accustomed to bending your knees. It will also help you to develop a good sense of balance.

Make a bridge with three poles as shown in the photograph. Make as many bridges as you can, placing them in a line from the top to the bottom of the practice hill. Ski down the hill, squatting down to pass under the bridge, and standing up until you approach the next bridge.

You can make this a little more difficult if you put the bridges in a zig-zag line down the hill. Then you will have to make turns between the bridges.

For all the exercises mentioned above, it is best to use a gentle hill with a wide open slope.

Practice all these maneuvers until you can do them easily.

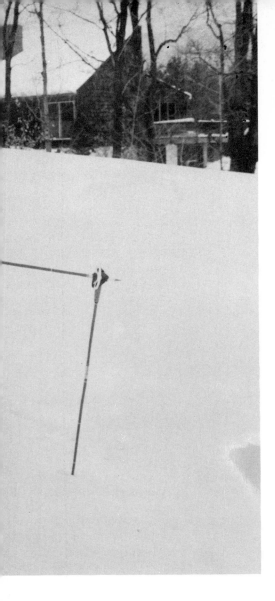

Skiing under a bridge of poles is fun and gives practice in flexing your knees and developing your sense of balance. Each bridge requires three poles. Make as many bridges as you can. Remain standing upright until you approach a bridge. Squat down to pass under it. Stand up again until you approach the next bridge.

7 | IMPROVING YOUR TECHNIQUE

After you have learned the basic techniques described in the preceding chapters, you will be ready for the fun of exploring ski touring trails, open fields, hiking trails, and other more challenging terrain.

Plan your first trips according to your physical condition. Take it easy in the beginning. If you haven't been getting too much exercise lately, it might be a mistake to tackle a trail that offers a lot of uphill climbing and steep downhill runs.

It won't be too long, though, before you can take on more challenging trails. Ski touring is a great way of improving your physical condition. It's an excellent all-around exercise for all: young and old, male and female. The condition of

This skier has spread her skis a comfortable distance apart to aid in retaining her balance during a fast downhill run.

your muscles and your respiratory and circulatory systems is bound to improve if you go touring regularly.

Handling Downhill Runs: On just about any trip, you will probably find steep slopes which will allow you to pick up a good deal of speed. As an aid in

This skier is facing a bumpy downhill run and has moved one ski about a foot ahead of the other. This is called the Telemark position. Note that her knees are flexed, her back straight, the tips of her poles just off the snow, and that she is looking ahead.

maintaining your balance while running downhill over such terrain, you might find it useful to assume a stance slightly wider than normal. That is, keep your skis a bit farther apart than usual.

When running downhill remember to keep your knees slightly bent and your weight balanced between the balls of your feet and your heels. Hold your poles away from your body with your hands slightly in front. Keep the baskets of your poles behind you, just off the snow.

When skiing through a wooded, bushy area, hold your poles by their handles only—don't use the pole straps. Then if the baskets should catch on a tree or a bush as you ski past, you can avoid being jolted off balance—which is what would happen if you had placed the straps around your wrists. Instead, you simply let go of the pole, stop, retrieve your pole, and continue your downhill run.

If you want to increase your speed on a downhill run, you can squat down to decrease your wind resistance. If you really want to pick up a lot of speed and you are facing a lengthy downhill run, you can rub ordinary paraffin wax on the bottoms of your skis, over the running wax, providing conditions are such that

you are using a hard running wax. Make sure, though, that you can see far enough ahead to avoid obstacles—or other people. Make sure, too, that your speed is under control. This means that you should always be able to turn or stop just where you wish. If you discover that you are running downhill too fast, slow down by snowplowing or turning until your speed is once again under control.

Handling Bumpy Terrain: Sooner or later, you will find downhill stretches which are quite bumpy. When you run across these bumps at any speed at all, you might find it a little harder to keep your balance than when you're skiing over a smooth surface.

You will find using the Telemark position useful in retaining your balance when skiing over bumps. All this means is that you slide one ski 8 to 10 inches ahead of the other. Keep your weight evenly divided between the two skis, and along the entire lengths of the skis. Keep your knees flexed; they will act as shock absorbers and reduce the jolt as you go over the bumps. The photo shows a skier in this position.

Proper touring technique is a smooth, rhythmic slight exaggeration of the walking stride—with a glide added to each forward motion. This skier is planting his left pole even with his right boot, his weight is over his right, or gliding, ski.

Developing Your Kick: You will be able to glide farther with each kick if you learn to make a complete weight shift each time you weight and unweight your skis. Thus, all your weight will be on the ski which is gliding forward. To accomplish this successfully, your upper torso will have to move from one side to the other as you glide forward on (and shift weight to) alternate skis.

It is also helpful to kick off with a sharp, definite pushing motion. As you develop skill in kicking, the tail of your kicking ski will be lifted off the snow as a result of a powerful kick and proper follow-through: after the kick, the follow-through movement of your leg describes an arc. At the completion of the arc, before it is brought forward for another kick, your leg extends out behind you, and is almost straight.

As you glide forward, first on one ski, then the other, remember to keep your knee bent and centered over the ski which is gliding. When you kick, the thrust is from the ball of the foot doing the kicking.

The factors that help you to kick backward with your skis in order to glide forward are the proper wax and the correct placement of your ski on the snow during your kick. This means that: a) the ski is flat on (or parallel to the surface of) the snow, and is not tilted to one side, and b) your weight is evenly distributed

along the length of the ski when you kick. This permits the maximum amount of wax to come into contact with the snow, which gives your ski the maximum amount of grip, or bite, on the snow.

Another point to remember is to keep in motion. That is, before you stop gliding on your weighted ski, kick off sharply with the other ski, which continues your forward motion. Don't wait until you come to a stop before kicking off again.

It is easy to overemphasize the kick when you are learning ski touring techniques. That is, although your kick should be a strong one, it should not be the dominating action of the technique. Beginners frequently tend to exaggerate the kick motion. This results in very jerky motions, loss of coordination with the arm movements, and improper balance. Think of touring technique as an exaggeration of a walking stride—with a glide added to each forward step. The touring stride is a natural one, and although each movement of arms and legs is described separately in this book, it is important to remember that we are describing the individual parts of a whole. When put together, these parts blend into one another and become a natural, graceful, and relaxed ground-eating movement.

The component parts of your touring technique are: 1) shift your weight, 2) bend your knee, keeping your ski flat on the snow and your weight centered on the ski, 3) kick off, and 4) pole to help your forward movement.

Poling: Try kicking along without the use of poles. You'll find it a bit difficult at first, but it is a great way to develop a more effective, efficient kick.

Diagonal poling, the only method discussed so far, is a very efficient method of helping to extend the distance you can glide with each kick. Any motion, however, can be tiring if continually repeated. You can avoid fatigue by changing

Striding along without the use of poles is useful in developing a strong, efficient kick.

to a different sequence of movements (and a different set of muscles) occasionally.

For this reason, you may wish to learn how to double pole during downhill runs and when skiing across flat areas. Double poling cannot be used when skiing uphill.

Double poling is simple: plant both poles, forward of your boots, at the same time. Push with them, hard, and follow through. That is, bend forward at your waist as you continue your push. When you do this, your hands will travel downward and back, past your knees. Then, raise up, swing your poles forward for another pole plant and repeat the process. There is nothing especially tricky about this; it is just another way of skiing across country.

Arm Movements: As with any other physical activity involving the use of your arms (such as golf or tennis), follow-through is important to efficient touring techniques. As you develop skill in gliding along on skis, you will find that you will glide farther and with less effort if you remember to follow through.

Thus, a diagonal pole plant begins with your arm, and your pole, swinging forward, ready for the pole plant. As you plant your pole, your elbow will be bent and your hand will be slightly higher than it would be if you were merely walking along. Indeed, your arm swing will be a slightly exaggerated, more vigorous version of the arm movement of a brisk walking stride. The tip of your pole will be planted in the snow as far forward as your opposite boot. As you push backward with your pole, push with a fair amount of force. As you glide by your planted pole, your arm gradually straightens out and you can relax your grip until you bring that arm forward again for the next pole plant.

8 | PLANNING YOUR TOURING TRIP

Very often, a little research during the summer will pay off when the snow season rolls around. If you are interested in discovering new territory and exploring new areas, you may want to hike or ride along old trails and roads and scout out places which might be suitable for touring.

Old, abandoned roads are excellent. So are the rough-cut logging roads through the woods. Rights of way for power and telephone lines are frequently suitable, as are the roadbeds of abandoned railroads. City parks and golf courses—provided you obtain permission to use them—are also good.

During the summer you will have plenty of time to get permission from property owners to ski over their property after the snow has fallen. You'll find that it pays to respect the rights of property owners. Treat their property as you would your own, and don't litter. Cave explorers have a saying which also applies to tourers: "Take nothing but pictures, leave nothing but footprints."

Other sources of valuable information on touring routes are road maps, government survey maps, and hiking trail maps. The Ski Touring Council's list of trails is also useful, if you live in the area included in the list.

Not too much planning is necessary for a short trip of an hour or so across a golf course or a familiar trail. More planning is necessary if you are interested in a longer trip. Pre-planning becomes increasingly important as your trips become longer.

For example, if the beginning and the end of the trail you plan to use are a good distance from each other, it is a good idea to use two automobiles. Leave one at the exit, then travel with your companions to the beginning of the trail. Thus, when your trip is completed, you will avoid a long walk back to your starting point.

It makes sense, on a long trip, to have at least three in your touring party. Four would be even better. If one of you should run into serious difficulty, one of your party could stay with him and the third and fourth could ski out and get help.

Several Alpine ski areas have made touring trails available. Most of these require that you sign in at the front desk or at the ski patrol desk before using their trails. This is for your own safety. If you don't return from your trip after a reasonable length of time, someone will come and look for you. It is wise to inform someone of your route even if it isn't required—no matter where you plan to go. Thus, if you run into trouble, you will know that eventually someone will come looking for you.

Get into the habit of carrying a spare ski tip. These metal or plastic gadgets fit over the end of a broken ski and make it much easier to continue your trip should you break a ski.

It can be helpful to carry a wax kit, in case snow conditions change during your trip, or if your wax needs touching up. A small waxing torch is also useful. So is a short screwdriver to tighten loose binding screws. The Østbye/Bass scraper can also be used for tightening screws.

If you plan to travel into sparsely populated areas, or the deep woods, carry a compass and a few matches.

Don't forget to bring along an extra-heavy sweater or jacket. Put it on when you stop, even for a few minutes. Remove it when you resume skiing.

As you ski along, you're likely to get pretty warm, even in cold weather. The trick in staying comfortable is to remove layers of clothing and open up zippers *before* you get all sweaty and steamy, not after. If your sweater is all wet with sweat, and you take it off, it's likely to freeze and will be useless for the rest of the trip. Similarly, when you stop for lunch or a rest put on your spare sweater or jacket *before* you begin to feel cold. Once you learn to regulate your body heat, it will become an automatic process, which will result in your being comfortable regardless of the outside temperature.

Even on a short trip, a thermos of hot chocolate or sweetened tea will be welcome. The best kinds of foods to take with you are the high energy, low weight foods: raisins, nuts, chocolate bars. It never hurts to stick a couple of extra chocolate bars in your pack before a trip. Of course, if you're planning a day-long trip, you'll need more food than for a jaunt of an hour or two. Don't underestimate the amount of energy you'll be using; bring plenty of food.

Generally, the items you should carry with you depend a good deal on where you're going and how long you'll be gone. Try to find out in advance the kind of terrain over which you'll be traveling and carry the appropriate equipment to insure that your trip will be a safe and successful one.

After a few short outings on touring skis, you might also become interested in going off into the real wilderness. This sort of trip begins to approach the area of ski mountaineering, and it is an entirely different thing from a casual three- or four-mile trip. Should mountaineering appeal to you, there are several good books on the subject.

If you know an area well and if the spirit so moves you, there is no real reason why you can't enjoy a night trip on skis. Night trips should be limited to bright moonlit nights and only during fine weather. Be sure each person brings a flashlight. Don't plan too ambitiously for night trips: make sure you're familiar with the terrain and stay with your planned route.

Whether your trips are made during the day or night, make sure you obtain a reliable weather forecast before you start out. It is annoying to have to ski through a snow storm, particularly if you're not sure of the landmarks along the route. Pay close attention to the forecast for wind. No matter what the actual temperature, the *effective* temperature will be lower when it is windy, in direct proportion to the velocity of the wind. Thus, the windier it is, the colder it will seem.

Finally, whatever the terrain or distance might be on any trip, remember to ski within your physical limits. Touring is for fun; overexerting yourself isn't. For instance, if you come to a hill too steep for you to ski down, sidestep down. Don't try to be a hero and ski beyond your capabilities. If you find yourself going too fast on a downhill stretch, slow down. Use a snowplow, or a turn, or squat down and drag your hands in the snow, or fall if all else fails (remember to fall uphill, not downhill). Keep your trips short and over undemanding trails at first. Build up your physical ability and your technical skills. Then you can venture further afield and you will eventually be able to ski over any kind of terrain.

9 | TAKING CARE OF YOUR EQUIPMENT

Touring equipment is simple and rugged and it will last for a long time, if you take care of it. There really is little except common sense involved in caring for your gear. First, let's look at what you should do during the skiing season to keep your equipment in top shape.

IN-SEASON CARE: Routine care of your gear will be easier to do on a regular basis if you remember two things: 1) Your skis and poles are made of wood and they can therefore absorb water and become splintered, gouged, or split if they are mishandled. 2) Your boots, if made of leather, are subject to the same kinds of problems that shorten the life of leather boots or shoes: drying, stiffening, and leaking.

Skis: Wipe the snow off your skis before you bring them indoors. First of all, you won't make such a mess in the house from melted snow. Secondly, trying to wax a wet ski is no fun. Thirdly, if you lean a snowy ski against a wall, and allow the snow to melt and run down to form a puddle on the floor, the ski will probably absorb some of this water, through the tail. Such absorption of water can cause the ski to warp out of shape. Also if a ski has absorbed water and you take it outside again, into the cold weather, the water within the ski will freeze and expand. The result will be a cracked or split ski.

After each trip, it's a good idea to look your skis over. If the binding screws are loose, tighten them up. Use a screwdriver with the proper sized blade—one which fills the screw slot completely.

Also look over the bottoms of your skis. If you find any gouges or splinters, fix them with plastic wood or smooth them out with sandpaper or a knife. Make sure the area you fill in with plastic wood is cleaned of any wax or other material that would prevent a good bond.

Boots: Take care of your touring boots as you would any footwear subject to rough use outdoors in winter. If they are made of leather, a waterproofing preparation should be applied often enough to prevent them from soaking up moisture. Don't dry the boots rapidly. This can make them curl. Keep a boot tree in them while they're not in use. If they get muddy during a trip, clean them when you get home.

Poles: Examine your poles periodically to make sure the baskets are in good shape and that the pins holding them to the pole shafts are securely fastened. If the bamboo shafts begin to split, wrap them with black plastic electricians' tape.

BETWEEN-SEASON STORAGE: Remember that even when your skis are stored for the summer they can absorb moisture and warp out of shape, or they can become dried out, which will make them brittle and easily broken. Store them in a cool, dry—but not too dry—spot. The best method is to lean them against a wall on their tips. Any good touring ski does not need to be blocked.

Look over your skis carefully before storing them. If the tops and sides are worn, refinish them with varnish or paint. Clean the bottoms of wax, then apply a light coat of base preparation.

Make sure your boots are polished and have boot trees in them for summer storage.

Finally, try to store your gear in one place. This will save a lot of searching when the snow begins to fall and the touring trails beckon.

APPENDIX:
WIND
CHILL
CHART

The chart reproduced here, courtesy of the U.S. Weather Service, shows how cold weather and wind can combine to produce a chilling effect far greater than the temperature alone. To read it, just determine the velocity of the wind and follow that line until you come to the temperature, in degrees Farenheit, under the temperature reading for the day. For instance, if the wind is blowing at 20 mph and the temperature is 20 degrees, the *effective* temperature is nine degrees below zero.

WIND MPH	TEMP. 35	30	25	20	15	10	5	−5	−10	−15	−20	−25	−30	−35
5	33	27	21	16	12	7	1	−6	−11	−15	−20	−26	−31	−35
10	21	16	9	2	−2	−9	−15	−22	−27	−31	−38	−45	−52	−58
15	16	11	1	−6	−11	−18	−25	−33	−40	−45	−51	−60	−65	−70
20	12	3	−4	−9	−17	−24	−32	−40	−46	−52	−60	−68	−76	−81
25	7	0	−7	−15	−22	−29	−37	−45	−52	−58	−67	−75	−83	−89
30	5	−2	−11	−18	−26	−33	−41	−49	−56	−63	−70	−78	−87	−94
35	3	−4	−13	−20	−27	−35	−43	−52	−60	−67	−72	−83	−90	−98
40	1	−4	−15	−22	−29	−36	−45	−54	−62	−69	−76	−87	−94	−101